# Take a Breath, Heather

By Clem King

Heather woke up with a heavy feeling in her tummy, but she was not sick.

She wished she could just go back to sleep, but she was not sleepy.

Instead, she got dressed and headed down for breakfast.

"Good morning, Heather!" called Dad.

Heather didn't answer him.

Heather toasted some bread and spread some jam on it, but she was not hungry.

“Get ready, Heather!” called Dad. “We might miss the bus!”

Heather dragged herself up and grabbed her backpack. She put her arms into the straps. The backpack felt so heavy, like it was full of lead!

Dad and Heather headed to the bus stop.

The sky was grey and cloudy. Even the weather suited her mood!

“What’s up, Heather?” asked Dad. “You are very quiet this morning.”

“I have to give a book report to the class!” cried Heather. “I’m dreading it!”

"Have you read the book?" asked Dad.

"Yes, I read it," said Heather.

"Did you write the report?" asked Dad.

"Yes!" said Heather.

“Then what’s the problem?” asked Dad.

“I have to get up and talk in front of all my classmates!” Heather cried.
“I will start to sweat and shake.”

I don't think speaking in front of a crowd is pleasant for anyone. Try taking a deep breath – it'll help you feel steady.

"I think I have a pain in my head!" said Heather.

"You are very healthy," Dad laughed. "You are ready! Just take a breath, Heather."

Dad met Heather after school.

“How did the talk go?” asked Dad.

“It was great!” cried Heather.
“I took a big breath and gave my book report.”

“I’m so proud of you!” said Dad.

Heather felt as light as a feather.
She leapt with joy!

## CHECKING FOR MEANING

1. What did Dad tell Heather she should do to feel steady before talking in front of her class? *(Literal)*
2. How did Heather feel at the end of the story? *(Literal)*
3. Why wasn't Heather hungry in the morning? *(Inferential)*
4. Do you think Dad gave Heather good advice? Why? *(Evaluative)*

## EXTENDING VOCABULARY

| | |
|---|---|
| **heavy** | What does it mean if Heather had a *heavy feeling in her tummy*? How might you feel if you have a heavy feeling in your tummy? |
| **lead** | Lead is a very heavy metal. Did Heather's backpack really have lead in it? What did the author mean when she said Heather's backpack felt *like it was full of lead?* |
| **dreading** | What does it mean if you are dreading something? Are you looking forward to it? |

## MOVING BEYOND THE TEXT

1. Have you ever been nervous about something? What did you do to help you feel calm?

2. If you had to write a book report, what book would you choose to write about? Why?

3. Heather and Dad rode the bus to school. How do you get to school?

4. Dad told Heather, *"You are ready!"* What would you say to someone who was feeling nervous? Has anyone ever helped you when you felt nervous?

## TIME TO WRITE

Write about a time you did something even though you were scared or nervous to do it.